The Grand Canyon: The History of the America's Most Famous Natural Wonder

By Charles River Editors

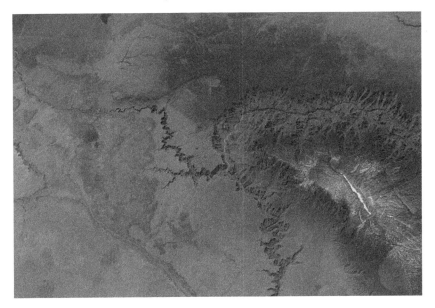

A satellite image of the Grand Canyon

About Charles River Editors

Charles River Editors provides superior editing and original writing services across the digital publishing industry, with the expertise to create digital content for publishers across a vast range of subject matter. In addition to providing original digital content for third party publishers, we also republish civilization's greatest literary works, bringing them to new generations of readers via ebooks.

Sign up here to receive updates about free books as we publish them, and visit Our Kindle Author Page to browse today's free promotions and our most recently published Kindle titles.

Introduction

An aerial view of the Grand Canyon

The Grand Canyon

"The wonders of the Grand Canyon cannot be adequately represented in symbols of speech, nor by speech itself. The resources of the graphic art are taxed beyond their powers in attempting to portray its features. Language and illustration combined must fail...You cannot see the Grand Canyon in one view, as if it were a changeless spectacle from which a curtain might be lifted, but to see it, you have to toil from month to month through its labyrinths." – John Wesley Powell

Even for those who have never seen it, the Grand Canyon is perhaps the most appreciated and remarkable feature of the American landscape. Indeed, the Grand Canyon has been amazing Americans since explorers first started venturing into the area in the mid-19th century. On one expedition, May Humphreys Stacey wrote in his journal of "a wonderful canyon four thousand feet deep. Everyone (in the party) admitted that he never before saw anything to match or equal this astonishing natural curiosity."

Cut through by the Colorado River over the course of millions of years, the Grand Canyon is a popular destination spot that attracts millions of tourists annually, and what they come to see can be found nowhere else on the planet. Whether they ride donkeys across steep ledges or visit old Pueblo settlements in the area (which the natives themselves considered a holy site), awe-inspiring spectacles abound. As Jack Schmitt put it, "It's like trying to describe what you feel when you're standing on the rim of the Grand Canyon or remembering your first love or the birth of your child. You have to be there to really know what it's like."

Of course, while most people marvel at its beauty, the Grand Canyon is an invaluable scientific boon for researchers who are given access to various layers of sediment, which provides all kinds of information about the past. The area is also home to countless species of plants and animals, and due to the nature of the terrain and the varying heights, the Grand Canyon has several different ecosystems within it. President Roosevelt recognized its importance after visiting it in the early 20th century, and his administration helped to preserve the Grand Canyon by turning it into a preserve. A decade later, Woodrow Wilson ensured that it was designated as a National Park.

The Grand Canyon: The History of the America's Most Famous Natural Wonder chronicles the history of America's most famous physical wonder. Along with pictures of important people, places, and events, you will learn about the Grand Canyon like never before, in no time at all.

The Grand Canyon: The History of the America's Most Famous Natural Wonder

About Charles River Editors

Introduction

Chapter 1: Its Carrying Power is Enormous

A picture of fog filling the Grand Canyon

"The Colorado River is unlike any other great river in the world. For present purposes it seems to be almost useless. In a large part of its course it drains an arid country which needs every drop of water thus carried away. It is, therefore, a vampire curse instead of a fructifying blessing. It is inaccessible to the general traveler, who, standing on its banks and gazing upon its far-away stream, yet perishes with agonizing thirst. No ordinary boat, whether propelled by oars, steam, or electricity, can live and either ascend or descend its turbulent waters. Practically no fish are found in its undisturbed solitudes. Though the country through which it flows is dreadfully arid, it is so unaccommodating as to refuse to be piped or pumped by any simple method to relieve the Sahara above. Though its carrying power is enormous, no commerce can place useful loads upon its rudely tossing back. Though its electric potentiality is great, it refuses to yield a single volt for any useful purpose. It is the wild, untamed, ferocious stallion of rivers, proud, self-willed, impetuous, powerful, wholly unrestrained and unrestrainable, yet attractive, grand, and majestic." - George Wharton James, *In & Around the Grand Canyon*

In the early 20th century, author George Wharton James decried the Colorado River in ways that would today seem unbelievable to any modern adventurer who has ever "shot the rapids" down the famous river. In 1900, however, that is very much as the river was perceived, for natural resources were seen as something to serve people's practical needs more than a need for fulfillment or exercise. This, of course, was primarily because so many Americans, especially those living in the West, experienced plenty of adventures and exercise just trying to survive.

Of course, there were always some people in the 19th century who sought the kind of excitement that is more commonplace now. One such man was John Wesley Powell, a Civil War veteran who became one of the first white men to visit the Grand Canyon in 1867. He later wrote, "Thousands of these little lakes, with deep, cold, emerald waters, are embosomed among the crags of the Rocky Mountains. These streams, born in the cold, gloomy solitudes of the upper mountain region, have a strange, eventful history as they pass down through gorges, tumbling in cascades and cataracts, until they reach the hot, arid plains of the Lower Colorado, where the waters that were so clear above, empty, as turbid floods, into the Gulf of California, in latitude 31° 53' and longitude 115°."

Powell

These "little lakes," joined by the river, provide some of the loveliest and most scenic places in the basin. They are well protected, and almost hidden from the world around them by mountains in excess of 10,000 feet above sea level. According to Powell, "All winter long, on its mountain-crested rim, snow falls, filling the gorges, half burying the forests, and covering the crags and peaks with a mantle woven by the winds from the waves of the sea, — a mantle of snow. When the summer sun comes, this snow melts, and tumbles down the mountain-sides in millions of cascades. Ten million cascade brooks unite to form ten thousand torrent creeks: ten thousand torrent creeks unite to form a hundred rivers beset with cataracts; a hundred roaring rivers unite to form the Colorado, which rolls a mad, turbid stream, into the Gulf of California."

Indeed, the river is much, much longer than the canyon that has made it famous, stretching nearly 2,000 miles from its head in the Wind River Mountains in Wyoming to its mouth in the Gulf of California. As Powell explained, "The area of country drained by the Colorado and its tributaries is about eight hundred miles in length, and varies from three to five hundred in width, containing about three hundred thousand square miles, — an area larger than all the New England and Middle States, with Maryland and Virginia added, or as large as Minnesota, Wisconsin, Iowa, Illinois, and Missouri."

It was, of course, the eternal action of the Colorado River that first cut and still continues to shape what it known today as the Grand Canyon. As George Wharton James put it, "It will readily be seen that these waters, dashing down to the sea, laden with rock debris, possess a power of corrosion far in excess of any ordinary river, and, as a result, each of these upper and side streams, as well as the Colorado itself, cuts deeper, and deeper, and deeper still into the rocks through which lie their beds, until their sides are towering cliffs of solid rocks." Powell had expressed a similar sentiment as well: "For more than a thousand miles along its course, the Colorado has cut for itself such a canyon; but at some few points, where lateral streams join it, the canyon is broken, and narrow, transverse valleys divide it properly into a series of canyons [including Horseshoe Canyon] where the river takes a course directly into the mountain, penetrating to its very heart, then wheels back upon itself, and runs out into the valley from which it started only half a mile below the point at which it entered, thus forming an elongated letter U, with the apex in the center of the mountain;"

Pictures that indicate how steep the canyons can be in certain places

Of course, Horseshoe Canyon is a mere child compared to the Grand Canyon itself, which begins at the mouth of the Little Colorado and extends more than 200 miles to the Grand Wash. C. E. Dutton, writing in the latter half of the 19th Century, noted, "The name, the Grand Canyon, has been repeatedly infringed for purposes of advertisement. The Canyon of the Yellowstone has been called 'The Grand Canyon.' A more flagrant piracy is the naming of the gorge of the Arkansas River in Colorado 'The Grand Canyon of Colorado/ and many persons who have visited it have been persuaded that they have seen the great chasm. These river valleys are certainly very pleasing and picturesque, but there is no more comparison between them and the mighty chasm of the Colorado River than there is between the Alleghenies or Trosachs and the Himalayas. Those who have long and carefully studied the Grand Canyon of the Colorado do not hesitate for a moment to pronounce it by far the most sublime of all earthly spectacles. If its sublimity consisted only in its dimensions, it could be sufficiently set forth in a single sentence. It is more than two hundred miles long, from five to twelve miles wide, and from five thousand to six thousand feet deep. There are in the world valleys which are longer and a few which are deeper. There are valleys flanked by summits loftier than the palisades of the Kaibab. Still the Grand Canyon is the sublimest thing on earth. It is so not alone by virtue of its magnitudes, but by virtue of the whole — its tout ensemble. The common notion of a canyon is that of a deep, narrow gash in the earth, with nearly vertical walls, like a great and neatly cut trench. There are hundreds of chasms in the Plateau Country (the country drained by the Colorado River) which answer very well to this notion. Many of them are sunk to frightful depths and are fifty to a hundred miles in length. Some are exceedingly narrow, as the canyons of the forks of the Virgen, where the over- hanging walls shut out the sky. Some are intricately sculptured, and illuminated with brilliant colors; others are picturesque by reason of their bold and striking sculptures. A few of them are most solemn and impressive by reason of their profundity and the majesty of their walls."

Dutton then went on to describe what made the Grand Canyon so unique among the important natural wonders of the world: "But, as a rule, the common canyons are neither grand nor even attractive upon first acquaintance. They are curious and awaken interest as a new sensation, but they soon grow tiresome for want of diversity, and become at last mere bores. The impressions they produce are very transient because of their great simplicity and the limited range of ideas they present. But there are some which are highly diversified, presenting many attractive features. These seldom grow stale or wearisome, and their presence is generally greeted with pleasure. It is perhaps in some respects unfortunate that the stupendous pathway of the Colorado River through the Kaibabs was ever called a canyon, for the name identifies it with the baser conception. But the name presents as wide a range of signification as the word house. The log-cabin of the rancher, the painted and vine-clad cottage of the mechanic, the home of the millionaire, the palaces where parliaments assemble, and the grandest temples of worship are all * houses.' Yet the contrast between St. Mark's and the rude dwelling of the frontiersman is not greater than that between the chasm of the Colorado and the trenches in the rocks which answer to the ordinary conception of a canyon. And as a great cathedral is an immense development of the rudimentary idea involved in the four walls and roof of a cabin, so is the chasm an expansion of the simple type of drainage channels peculiar to the Plateau Country. To the conception of its vast proportions must be added some notion of its intricate plan, the nobility of its architecture, its colossal buttes, its wealth of ornamentation, the splendor of its colors, and its wonderful atmosphere. All of these attributes combine with infinite complexity to produce a whole which at first bewilders and at length overpowers."

The view from Moran Point

Chapter 2: Falls, Cataracts, and Rapids

"The Grand Canyon District, which lies in the arid region of southern Utah and northern Arizona, contains an area which is roughly estimated at from thirteen thousand to sixteen thousand square miles, or about the size of the State of Maryland. In this district there are, in less than five hundred miles, five hundred and twenty falls, cataracts, and rapids. This district is arbitrarily divided into various canyons as before stated." - George Wharton James, *In & Around the Grand Canyon*

Over the years, millions of people have visited the Grand Canyon, but few if any have ever been prepared for what they saw when they first arrived. Even more than a century ago, James observed, "A canyon indeed it truly is, but entirely different from what all visitors' expect to see. It is not a deep, narrow, gloomy gorge, into which the sun fails to shine even at midday. It is, in reality, a series of canyons one within and below the other. Picture one canyon, a thousand feet deep and ten or twelve miles across; below this, another canyon, but two miles less in width and a thousand feet deeper than number one; then, still another, two thousand feet deeper and four miles narrower, followed by yet another, deeper still and more miles narrower, until the inner gorge of granite is reached, through which the roaring river flows, and you will have a better idea than ever before."

One of the things that makes the Grand Canyon so beautiful is its wide variety of rock formations. The earliest Native American Tribes to visit it, including the Hopi, Paiute and Havasupai, knew of it as a place rimmed by a layer of limestone hundreds of feet thick, under which were layers of sandstone. One of the layers had a traditional creamy color, and the other had a reddish hue. Below that could be seen granite or other Subcarboniferous rocks. Mining engineer Robert Brewster Stanton once wrote, "Cataract and Narrow Canyons are wonderful, Glen Canyon is beautiful, Marble Canyon is mighty; but it is left for the Grand Canyon, where the river has cut its way down through the sandstones, the marbles, and the granites of the

Kaibab Mountains, to form those beautiful and awe- inspiring pictures that are seen from the bottom of the black granite gorge, where above us rise great wondrous mountains of bright red sandstone, capped with cathedral domes and spires of white, with pinnacles, and turrets, and towers in such intricate form and flaming colors that words fail to convey any idea of their beauty and sublimity."

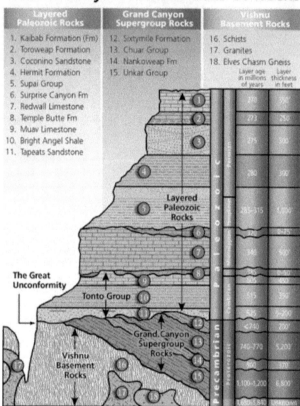

Grand Canyon's Three Sets of Rocks

Layered Paleozoic Rocks	Grand Canyon Supergroup Rocks	Vishnu Basement Rocks
1. Kaibab Formation (Fm)	12. Sixtymile Formation	16. Schists
2. Toroweap Formation	13. Chuar Group	17. Granites
3. Coconino Sandstone	14. Nankoweap Fm	18. Elves Chasm Gneiss
4. Hermit Formation	15. Unkar Group	
5. Supai Group		
6. Surprise Canyon Fm		
7. Redwall Limestone		
8. Temple Butte Fm		
9. Muav Limestone		
10. Bright Angel Shale		
11. Tapeats Sandstone		

An image depicting the stratigraphy of the Grand Canyon

A picture demonstrating some of the different colors

A picture of old Pueblo settlements

The "Pathfinder" himself, John C. Fremont, noted, "Three hundred miles of its lower part, as it approaches the Gulf of California, is reported to be smooth and tranquil; but its upper part is manifestly broken into many falls and rapids. From many descriptions of trappers, it is probable that in its foaming course among its lofty precipices it presents many scenes of wild grandeur; and though offering many temptations, and often discussed, no trappers have been found bold enough to undertake a voyage which has so certain a prospect of a fatal termination. The Indians have strange stories of beautiful valleys abounding with beaver, shut up among inaccessible walls of rock in the lower course of the river, and to which the neighboring Indians, in their occasional wars with the Spaniards, and among themselves, drive their herds of cattle and flocks of sheep, leaving them to pasture in perfect security."

Fremont

In fact, back in the latter half of the 19th century scientist T. Mitchell Prudden complained about the challenges the canyon posed to drawing state boundaries: "The Grand and Marble Canyons cut the northwestern corner of Arizona completely off from the rest of the Territory. Except by Lee's Ferry, and the long hot road which leads to it, or by a far western route, this corner is inaccessible from the south. It looks small enough on the map, but it is rather larger than the State of Connecticut, and, save for a few scattered cattle-shacks, has no human habitation."

Of course, such distinctions were never a concern until America's westward expansion. When Spanish explorers traveling through the area in 1540 became the first Europeans to see the canyon, they were more interested in finding gold than a big hole in the ground. As James later put it, "In less than fifty years after the landing of Columbus on the shores of the Western Hemisphere, Spanish explorers and missionaries were travelling upon the Colorado River, following its course a long way from its mouth, reaching it at various points, and even visiting it on the east side of its junction with the Colorado Chiquito, — the Little Colorado, — which, to this day, is one of its most inaccessible points. These Spanish explorations were largely the result of that never to be forgotten first transcontinental journey, made on foot by Don Alvar Nunez Cabeza de Vaca, the unfortunate treasurer of the ill-fated expedition of Panfilo de Narvaez to the coast of Florida. The stories of what he saw and heard aroused the viceroy of New Spain (Northern Mexico) to send out a preliminary reconnaissance party under the direction of a trustworthy Franciscan friar, Marcos de Niza. Marcos penetrated Arizona and went east as far as the now known pueblos of Zuni, in New Mexico. These, he was told, were the seven cities of Cibola. On his favor- able report being presented to the viceroy, a large and imposing expedition, under the command of that young, handsome, adventurous, wealthy, and favored caballero, Don Vazquez de Coronado, was sent forward to explore, subjugate, and possess the new lands in the name of God and the King of Spain."

Don Alvar Nunez Cabeza de Vaca

One of the soldiers, Ensign Tobar, heard of a "large river," and according to Pedro de Castañeda of Najera, the author of *The Journey of Coronado, 1540–1542* (1596), "As Don Pedro de Tobar was not commissioned to go farther, he returned from there and gave this information to the general, who dispatched Don Garcia Lopez de Cardenas with about twelve companions to go to see this river. He was well received when he reached Tusayan, and was entertained by the natives, who gave him guides for his journey. They started from here loaded with provisions, for they had to go through a desert country before reaching the inhabited region, which the Indians said was more than twenty days' journey. After they had gone twenty days they came to the banks of the river, which seemed to be more than three or four leagues above the stream which flowed between them."

Thus, Coronado started out on land while Mendoza sailed along the coast until he reach what is now called the Gulf of California. According to 19th century historian George Parker Winship, the leaders, seeing that they were at the mouth of what was obviously a large river, took "twenty men in two boats [and] started upstream on Thursday, August 26, 1540, when white men for the first time floated on the waters of the Colorado. The Indians appeared on the river banks during the following day. The silence with which the strangers answered the threatening shouts of the natives, and the presence of the Indian interpreters in the boats, soon overcame the hostile attitude of the savages. The European trifles which had been brought for gifts and for trading completed the work of establishing friendly relations, and the Indians soon became so well disposed that they entirely relieved the Spaniards of the labor of dragging the boats up the stream. A crowd of Indians seized the ropes by which the boats were hauled against the current, and from this time on some of them were always ready to render this service to their visitors. In this fashion the Spaniards continued northward, receiving abundant supplies of corn from the natives, whose habits and customs they had many excellent opportunities for observing. Alarcon [one of the leaders] instructed these people dutifully in the worship of the cross, and continually questioned them about the places whose names Friar Marcos had heard.' He met with no success until he had travelled a considerable distance up the river, when for the first time he found a man with whom his interpreter was able to converse."

Frederic Remington's painting depicting Coronado's journey into North America

Hearing that Coronado was nearby, the men tried to get word to him but ultimately failed to do so. As a result, they sailed back down the river to rejoin the other ships. Winship continued, "Starting September 14, [Alarcon] found the Indians as friendly as before, and ascended the river, as he judged, about 85 leagues, which may have taken him to the point where the canyons begin. A cross was erected to inform Coronado, in case an expedition from Cibola should reach this part of the river, that he had tried to fulfil his duty, but nothing more was accomplished."

Two centuries passed before Padre Consag was able to travel up the Colorado River from the Gulf of California to its mouth, and another century later, the United States Army of the West crossed the Colorado River on its way to California. Yet another decade passed before a Lieutenant Amiel Weeks Whipple surveyed the lower part of the Grand Canyon itself, and around the same time, the inscription "I Julien, 1836" was found deeply carved into the rock face near the edge of the river. F. A. Nims, *Through Mysterious Cañons of the Colorado*, photographed the carving and later said, "As it could only have been done from the water by someone either in a boat or on a raft, the only solution we could arrive at was that it was done by one of a party of Canadian voyagers, which is reported to have attempted to explore this part of the country in 1836 — thirty-three years before Major Powell and his party made their memorable trip, and fifty-three years before we followed. What became of them I have been unable to ascertain. No written account has ever been published of their journey."

Whipple

Powell himself referred to an earlier expedition when he wrote, "On a high rock by which the trail passes we find the inscription: 'Ashley 18-5. The third figure is obscure — some of the party reading it 1835, some 1855. James Baker, an old-time mountaineer, once told me about a party of men starting down the river, and Ashley was named as one. The story runs that the boat was swamped, and some of the party drowned in one of the canyons below. The word 'Ashley' is a warning to us, and we resolve on great caution. Ashley Falls is the name we give to the cataract we have just passed. Eight days later we discover an iron bake oven, several tin plates, a part of a boat, and many other fragments, which denote the spot where Ashley's party came to disaster and, possibly, death."

In 1857, the federal government sent an expedition to explore the Colorado River and determine whether it could be used to transport military supplies. Lieutenant Joseph Ives later wrote of his first impressions of the Grand Canyon, "It looks like the Gates of Hell. The region ... is, of course, altogether valueless. Ours has been the first and will undoubtedly be the last, party of whites to visit the locality. It seems intended by nature that the Colorado River along the greater portion of its lonely and majestic way, shall be forever unvisited and undisturbed."

James made reference to Ives' sentiment about a decade later: "Up to [the late 1860s] it will be seen that no adequate survey of the Colorado River or its canyons had been made. Exploring parties or individuals had touched it here and there, but there had been no thorough and satisfactory exploration. It was left to the untiring energy, persistent zeal, and scientific instincts of Major J. W. Powell to accomplish the impossible; for Indians, miners, prospectors, cowboys, Spanish explorers, and United States government officers were a unit in saying that it was a practical impossibility to ride down the Colorado River from its source to its mouth. Exaggerated stories of Ives' report reached the ears of the miners, prospectors, and hunters who wandered into the country, and these, in time, started other stories equally exciting, which aroused much interest and curiosity, although it is doubtful whether any of them had much, if any, foundation in fact." - George Wharton James, *In & Around the Grand Canyon*

Chapter 3: To Rightly Enjoy It

"The canyon through which this muddy, salt stream flows is on a scale quite as grand, although not so extensive, as that of the Colorado itself. Standing on Paiuti Point (Grand View) near the Grand View Trail, the cliffs above the mouth of the Little Colorado are distinctly to be seen; but to rightly enjoy it, one should ride around the rim, some thirty-five miles, and see the junction of the two rivers." - George Wharton James, *In & Around the Grand Canyon*

Scott Catron's picture of the North Rim

As exaggerated as they sound now, by the time Powell began exploring the Grand Canyon, Ives' words of caution were widely believed to be an accurate description of the terrors that awaited anyone who tried to explore the Grand Canyon. Powell later admitted, "Tales were told of parties entering the gorge in boats, and being carried down with fearful velocity into whirlpools, where all were overwhelmed in the abyss of waters; others, of underground passages for the great river, into which boats had passed never to be seen again. It was currently believed that the river was lost under the rocks for several hundred miles. There were other accounts of great falls, whose roaring music could be heard on the distant mountain summits. There were many stories current of parties wandering on the brink of the canyon, vainly endeavoring to reach the waters below, and perishing with thirst at last in sight of the river which was roaring its mockery into dying ears."

Powell's journey, though carefully documented, would become the stuff of legends itself, with many believing that he could not have made it through the entire canyon. That said, George Wharton James, one of Powell's contemporaries, accepted Powell's account as true: "In 1867 he began explorations of the canyons and gorges of the Upper Colorado, and as the result of these early efforts, a party was organized in 1869 for the complete exploration of the Colorado River from its source to its mouth. On the 24th of May, 1869, the party left Green River City, the prow of the boats turned to flow with the swift current into the unknown dangers and wonders ahead. Three of the boats were of oak, and one of pine, — each divided into compartments, some of which were water-tight to make the boats buoyant. They were loaded with rations deemed sufficient to last ten months, — clothing, ammunition, tools, and all necessary scientific instruments."

Powell himself repeated an oft told Native American tale about the origin of the Grand Canyon that suggested it was full of danger. "The Indians, too, have woven the mysteries of the canyons into the myths of their religion. Long ago, there was a great and wise chief, who mourned the death of his wife, and would not be comforted until Ta-vwoats, one of the Indian gods, came to him, and told him she was in a happier land, and offered to take him there, that he might see for himself, if, upon his return, he would cease to mourn. The great chief promised. Then Ta-vwoats made a trail through the mountains that intervene between that beautiful land, the balmy region in the Great West, and this, the desert home of the poor Nu-ma. "This trail was the Canyon Gorge of the Colorado. Through it he led him; and when they had returned, the deity exacted from the chief a promise that he would tell no one of the joys of that land, lest, through discontent with the circumstances of this world, they should desire to go to heaven. Then he rolled a river into the gorge, a mad, raging stream, that should engulf any that might attempt to enter thereby."

In Powell's own words, "Away to the south, the Uinta Mountains stretch in a long line; high peaks thrust into the sky, and snow-fields glittering like lakes of molten silver; and pine forests in somber green; and rosy clouds playing around the borders of huge, black masses; and heights and clouds, and mountains and snowfields, and forests and rock-lands are blended into one grand view."

According to his diary, the expedition traveled 62 miles in its first five days, reaching Flaming Gorge. Powell continued, "Seventy and one-third miles from Flaming Gorge the gate of the Canyon of Lodore is reached, in which a succession of rapids are found. This is our method of procedure at such places. The Emma Dean goes in advance; the other boats follow, in obedience to signals. When we approach a rapid, or what, on other rivers, would often be called a fall, I stand on deck to examine it, while the oarsmen back-water, and we drift on as slowly as possible.

If I can see a clear chute between the rocks, away we go; but if the channel is beset entirely across, we signal the other boats, pull to land, and I walk along the shore for closer examination. If this reveals no clear channel, hard work begins. We drop the boats to the very head of the dangerous place, and let them over by lines, or make a portage, frequently carrying both boats and cargoes over the rocks, or perhaps, only the cargoes, if it is safe to let the boats down. The waves caused by such falls in a river differ much from the waves of the sea. The water of an ocean wave merely rises and falls; the form only passes on, and form chases form unceasingly. A body floating on such waves merely rises and sinks, — does not progress unless impelled by wind or some other power. But here, the water of the wave passes on, while the form remains. The waters plunge down ten or twenty feet, to the foot of the fall ; spring up again in a great wave ; then down and up, in a series of billows, that gradually disappear in the more quiet waters below ; but these waves are always there, and you can stand above and count them."

Jonathan Lamb's panorama of Flaming Gorge and the reservoir there today

From this point, Powell entered into another exciting portion of the river: "A boat riding such, leaps and plunges along with great velocity. Now, the difficulty in riding over these falls, when the rocks are out of the way, is in the first wave at the foot. This will sometimes gather for a moment, heaping up higher and higher, until it breaks back. If the boat strikes it the instant after it breaks, she cuts through, and the mad breaker dashes its spray over the boat, and would wash us overboard did we not cling tight. If the boat, in going over the falls, chances to get caught in some side current, and is turned from its course, so as to strike the wave "broad-side on," and the wave breaks at the same instant, the boat is capsized. Still, we must cling to her, for, the water-tight compartments acting as buoys, she cannot sink; and so we go, dragged through the waves, until still waters are reached. We then right the boat, and climb aboard."

The next day, the expedition reached "a channel filled with dangerous rocks that break the waves into whirlpools and beat them into foam. …the boat strikes a rock, rebounds from the shock, careens, and fills the open compartment with water. Two of the men lose their oars; she swings around, and is carried down at a rapid rate, broadside on, for a few yards, and strikes amidships on another rock with great force, is broken quite in two, and the men are thrown into the river; the larger part of the boat floating buoyantly, they soon seize it, and down the river they drift, past the rocks for a few hundred yards to a second rapid, filled with huge boulders, where the boat strikes again, and is dashed to pieces, and the men and fragments are soon carried beyond my sight. Running along, I turn a bend, and see a man's head above the water, washed about in a whirlpool below a great rock. It is Frank Goodman, clinging to it with a grip upon which life depends. Coming opposite, I see Rowland trying to go to his aid from an island on which he has been washed. Soon, he comes near enough to reach Frank with a pole, which he extends toward him. The latter lets go the rock, grasps the pole, and is pulled ashore. Seneca Howland is washed farther down the island, and is caught by some rocks, and, though somewhat bruised, manages to get ashore in safety. This seems a long time, as I tell it, but it is quickly done. And now the three men are on the island, with a swift, dangerous river on either side, and a fall below."

Powell understandably named this place "Disaster Falls" before moving on. From there, "just before us, the canyon divides, a little stream coming down on the right, and another on the left, and we can look away up either of these canyons, through an ascending vista, to cliffs and crags and towers, a mile back, and two thousand feet overhead. To the right, a dozen gleaming cascades are seen. Pines and firs stand on the rocks, and aspens overhang the brooks. The rocks below are red and brown, set in deep shadows, but above, they are buff and vermilion, and stand in the sunshine. The light above, made more brilliant by the bright-tinted rocks, and the shadows below more gloomy by the sombre hues of the brown walls, increase the apparent depths of the canyons, and it seems a long way up to the world of sunshine and open sky, and a long way down to the bottom of the canyon glooms."

Soon, the party came to Echo Park, located at the end of the Canyon of Lodore. After that, they headed through Whirlpool Canyon, Island Park and Split Mountain Canyon to the mouth of the Uinta River. After another 280 miles or so, they reached the Colorado River proper, where Powell reported that the group had to reach a decision. "[T]here are great descents yet to be made, but, if they are distributed in rapids and short falls, as they have been hitherto, we shall be able to overcome them. But maybe we shall come to a fall in these canyons which we cannot pass, where the walls rise from the water's edge, so that we cannot land, and where the water is so swift that we cannot return. Such places have been found except that the falls were not so great but that we could run them in safety. How will it be in the future? So the men speculate over the serious probabilities in a jesting mood, and I hear Sumner remark, 'My idea is, we had better go slow, and learn to paddle.'"

Thus, they made slow progress through Cataract and Glen Canyons over the next day, before reaching Marble Canyon. Here, according to Powell, "The scenery is on a grand scale. The walls of the Canyon, twenty-five hundred feet high, are of marble, of many beautiful colors, and often polished by the waves, or far up the sides, where showers have washed the sands over the cliffs. At one place I have a walk, for more than a mile, on a marble pavement, all polished and fretted with strange devices, and embossed in a thousand fantastic patterns. Through a cleft in the wall the sun shines on this pavement, which gleams in iridescent beauty. I pass up the cleft. It is very narrow, with a succession of pools standing at higher levels as I go back. The water in these pools is clear and cool, coming down from springs. Then I return to the pavement which is but a terrace or bench, over which the river runs at its flood, but left bare at present. Along the pavement, in many places, are basins of clear water, in strange contrast to the red mud of the river. At length I come to the end of this marble terrace, and take again to the boat. Riding down a short distance, a beautiful view is presented. The river runs sharply to the cast, and seems enclosed by a wall, set with a million brilliant gems. What can it mean? Every eye is engaged, everyone wonders. On coming nearer, we find fountains bursting from the rock, high overhead, and the spray in the sunshine forms the gems which bedeck the wall. The rocks below the fountain are covered with mosses, and ferns, and many beautiful flowering plants. We name it Vasey's Paradise, in honor of the botanist who travelled with us last year. It rains again this afternoon. Scarcely do the first drops fall, when little rills run down the walls. As the storm comes on, the little rills increase in size, until great streams are formed. Although the walls of the canyon are chiefly limestone, the adjacent country is of red sandstone ; and now the waters, loaded with these sands, come down in rivers of bright red mud, leaping over the walls in innumerable cascades. It is plain now how these walls are polished in many places."

An 1872 picture of Marble Canyon taken during Powell's subsequent expedition in 1872

A modern picture of Marble Canyon

The group passed through Marble Canyon to reach the Colorado Chiquito (Little Colorado). At this point, the walls were only about 200 feet high, but by the time the group reached the deepest part of the Grand Canyon, the walls on either side of them would be more than 3,500 feet high. As they entered the deepest parts, Powell wrote, "An unknown river we have yet to explore. What falls there are, we know not; what rocks beset the channel, we know not. What walls rise over the river, we know not. The water is swift, the walls rise from the very edge of the river. They are composed of tiers of irregular shelves below, and above these, steep slopes to the foot of the marble cliffs. Soon after entering, the river runs across a dike. A dike is a fissure in the rocks, open to depths below, which has been filled with eruptive matter, and this, on cooling, was harder than the rocks through which the crevice was made, and, when these were washed away, the harder volcanic matter remained as a wall, and the river has cut a gateway through it several hundred feet high, and as many wide. The very next day, the softer series of rocks are left behind, — newer and more dangerous experiences clearly are before us, for we now enter the granite. Here the canyon is narrow and the water swifter. The walls are set on either side, with pinnacles and crags; and sharp, angular buttresses, bristling with wind- and wave-polished spires, extend far out into the river. The walls, now, are a mile in height, — a vertical distance difficult indeed to appreciate. Stand in any street with which you are familiar, lined with stores on either side for a full mile, and then imagine this immense mass of buildings extending this mile upwards, — and you can then begin to comprehend the grandeur of these rock walls."

The brave explorers moved on to a point where "[t]he river is very deep, the canyon very narrow, and still obstructed, so that there is no steady flow of the stream; but the waters wheel, and roll, and boil, and we are scarcely able to determine where we can go. Now, the boat is carried to the right, perhaps close to the wall; again, she is shot into the stream, and perhaps is dragged over to the other side, where, caught in a whirlpool, she spins about. We can neither land nor run as we please. The boats are entirely unmanageable; no order in their running can be preserved; now one, now another is ahead, each crew laboring for its own preservation. In such a place we come to another rapid. Two of the boats run it perforce. One succeeds in landing, but there is no foothold by which to make a portage, and she is pushed out again into the stream. The next minute a great, reflex wave fills the open compartment; she is water-logged, and drifts unmanageable. Breaker after breaker rolls over her, and one capsizes her. The men are thrown out; but they cling to the boat, and she drifts down some distance, alongside of us, and we are able to catch her. She is soon bailed out, and the men are aboard once more. One more day, and we come to a beautifully clear stream which we name Bright Angel Creek. This is nearly opposite the Bright Angel Trail."

A picture of part of the Bright Angel Trail

By this time, the group, though still long on courage, was short on supplies. Also, it had started to rain hard, making it all but impossible to stay dry. Still, James later wrote that the expedition went "gleefully on, and three or four days afterwards come to monuments of lava standing in the river. Most of them are low rocks, but some are shafts more than three hundred feet high."

Despite the height, the men decided to risk a climb up the canyon walls in the hopes of reaching the top and then being able to find a settlement. Sadly, this proved to be a deadly mistake. According to Powell, "I [later] learned that they had come to the Indian village almost starved and exhausted with fatigue. They were supplied with food, and put on their way to the settlements. Shortly after they had left, an Indian from the east side of the Colorado arrived at the village, and told them (the Shi-vwits) about a number of miners having killed a squaw in a drunken brawl, and no doubt these were the men. No person had ever come down the canyon; that was impossible; they were trying to hide their guilt. In this way he worked them into a great rage. They followed, surrounded the three unfortunate men in ambush, and filled them full of arrows."

With fewer men, the group was able to leave behind one of their boats, along with many of the items they had thus far collected, and move on. As if the misfortune wasn't enough, that very afternoon they ran into some of the worst falls yet. Luckily, this proved to be end of their troubles, as they were out of the Grand Canyon by noon the following day. Powell wrote, "The relief from danger and the joy of success are great. When he who has been chained by wounds to a hospital cot, until his canvas tent seems like a dungeon cell, until the groans of those who lie about, tortured with probe and knife, are piled up, a weight of horror on his ears that he cannot throw off, cannot forget, and until the stench of festering wounds and anesthetic drugs has filled the air with its loathsome burden, — when such an one at last goes out into the open field, what a world he sees! How beautiful the sky! how bright the sunshine! what floods of delicious music pour from the throats of birds! how sweet the fragrance of earth, and tree, and blossom! The first hour of convalescent freedom seems rich recompense for all pain, gloom, terror. Something like this are the feelings we experience tonight. Ever before us has been an unknown danger, heavier than immediate peril. Every waking hour passed in the Grand Canyon has been one of toil. We have watched with deep solicitude the steady disappearance of our scant supply of rations, and from time to time have seen the river snatch a portion of the little left, while we were a-hungered. And danger and toil were endured in those gloomy depths, where oft times the clouds hid the sky by day, and but a narrow zone of stars could be seen at night. Only during the few hours of deep sleep, consequent on hard labor, has the roar of the waters been hushed. Now the danger is over; now the toil has ceased; now the gloom has disappeared ; now the firmament is bounded only by the horizon ; and what a vast expanse of constellations can be seen! The river rolls by us in silent majesty; the quiet of the camp is sweet; our joy is almost ecstasy. We sit till long after midnight, talking of the Grand Canyon, talking of home, but chiefly talking of the three men who left us. Are they wandering in those depths, unable to find a way out? are they searching over the desert lands above for water? or are they nearing the settlements?"

A picture of the South Rim of the Grand Canyon

An 1872 picture of the Grand Canyon taken during Powell's subsequent expedition

Chapter 4: The Most Dangerous Rapids

"On the 12th of January, 1897, N. Galloway…accompanied by William Richmond, left near the State line of Wyoming and Utah…. In those frail, rude boats they journeyed fourteen hundred miles, emerging through the steep canyon walls on the 3d day of February, and on the 17th of that month completing the trip at the Needles. … As Galloway and Richmond reached the open country below the Grand Wash, they came upon the officers who had found the bodies of two men killed by a Paiuti Indian…. This officer requested them to allow their boats to be used to convey the bodies down to the Needles. They did so, and on their arrival sold the boats and returned to their homes in Utah. Some months later I was fortunate enough to arrive at Lee's Ferry, when Mr. Galloway was there with a new boat he had just built, with which he proposed going up the river to a placer gold claim he had located in Glen Canyon. After considerable persuasion he was prevailed upon to take me up the canyon to his gold claim, and also down Marble Canyon, to Soap Creek Rapids, one of the most dangerous rapids in the canyon and near which Frank Brown lost his life." - George Wharton James, *In & Around the Grand Canyon*

Martin St-Amant's picture of the Grand Canyon at sunset

While Powell was the most famous of the 19th century explorers to head into the Grand Canyon, he was not the last. In May 1889, Frank Brown and Robert Stanton led an expedition through the area because Brown "had conceived the idea of building a railroad through the canyons of the Colorado River, from some point in Colorado, by a water grade, down the Grand and Colorado Rivers to some point in Southern California, where the road could be feasibly taken across to the coast." This party was the first to record a unique type of wave that they called a "fountain." According to one man, "Where the river is broad, deep, and swift, the bottom seems to be covered with potholes in the sandstone, and to have great heaps of constantly changing quicksand mounds. This causes numberless cross-currents underneath the surface, and at times these seem to combine, resulting in an enormous up-shooting wave, which breaks through the surface of the water with a swish and roar that are appalling, and tosses anything it may strike. The noise these 'fountains' make is something between the boom of a cannon and the rush of an enormous sky-rocket, and they can be heard for a mile. They do not rise twice in the same place, but switch about so that it is impossible to avoid them."

A picture of Stanton rowing in the Grand Canyon during the expedition

After making it through this particularly rough patch, the trip continued uneventfully until July 10, when Brown and another man "undertook to run the first rapid, by the side of which was a great whirlpool. They were going safely along a neutral strip of water between the two, when an enormous up-shooting wave struck the boat in the middle, throwing it into the air, and pitching Brown into the whirlpool, and McDonald into the rapid. Both were powerful swimmers. McDonald struck out, calling to Brown, 'Come on.' Brown replied, 'All right,' and faced down the river. McDonald had now all he could do to care for himself. Three times he was thrown under by the terrific tossings of the mad waters, but he managed to reach a rock about six hundred yards below the scene of the mishap. Dragging himself out, he was horrified to see Brown still in the whirlpool. Frantically he gestured to the following boat. It recognized his signals, and dashed for the whirlpool, but too late. Brown had disappeared a few seconds before it reached him, and that river never gives up its dead."

Despite the tragedy, the expedition continued. Stanton explained, "In this world we are left but little time to mourn. We had work to do, and I determined if possible to complete the whole of that work. With this intention we started out next morning. Thursday, Friday, and Saturday we pushed on with our usual work, shooting through or portaging round twenty-four bad rapids, getting deeper and deeper between the marble walls. After a quiet rest on Sunday, Monday morning found us at the head of two very rough and rocky rapids. We portaged both of them. While the photographer and myself took our notes and pictures, the boats were to go on through the lower end of the second rapid to a sandbar, a half-mile below. It was easy walking for us along the bank. The first boat got down with difficulty, as the current beat hard against the left cliff. My boat was the next to start. I pushed it out from shore myself with a cheering word to the men, Hansbrough and Richards. It was the last they ever heard. The current drove them against the cliff, under an overhanging shelf. In trying to push away from the cliff the boat was upset. Hansbrough was never seen to rise. Richards, a powerful man, swam some distance downstream. The first boat started out to the rescue, but he sank before it reached him. Two more faithful and good men gone! Astonished and crushed by our sad loss, our force too small to portage our boats, and our boats entirely unfit for such work, I decided to abandon the trip, with then and there a determination, as soon as a new outfit could be secured, to return and complete our journey to the Gulf."

Stanton did indeed return in December 1889 and completed his trip in March 1890 when, he wrote, he and his men "emerged at the lower end of Grand Canyon March 17th, reached the end of the survey at tide-water April 26th, and, returning to Yuma, disbanded on April 30th. One boat was completely destroyed in Rapid No. 249; but only two sacks of provisions were lost in the whole journey. Thus had the two expeditions, considered as one, travelled by boat a distance of over fourteen hundred miles, had passed over — running nearly all of them — five hundred and twenty rapids, falls, and cataracts in less than five hundred miles, making a total fall of forty-five hundred feet, and had passed successfully through the dark canyons of one of the most tempestuous rivers of the world."

In the process of finishing the expedition and writing a report about it, Stanton provided vivid details of the Grand Canyon: "It is hoped that in this description there has not only been shown the entire practicability of the canyons of the Colorado River for railway purposes, both from an economical as well as a purely engineering point of view, but that there has also been some light cast upon the nature and possibilities of a portion of our great Western empire, which, to many, has been less known than the heart of Africa. On January 13th, we reached Point Retreat, where we left the canyon on our homeward march just six months before. We found our supplies, — blankets, flour, sugar, coffee, etc., which we had cached in the marble cave, all in good condition. From the head of the Colorado to Point Retreat we had encountered one hundred and forty-four rapids, not counting small draws, in a distance of two hundred and forty miles. From Lee's Ferry to Point Retreat there are forty-four rapids, in a distance of thirty miles. With our new boats we ran nearly all of these, and portaged but few; over many of them our boats had danced and jumped at the rate of fifteen miles an hour, and over some, by actual measurement, at the rate of twenty miles per hour. To stand in the bow of one of these boats as she dashes through a great rapid, with first the bow and then the stern jumping into the air, and the spray of the breakers splashing over one's head, is an excitement the fascination of which can only be understood through experience. Ten miles below Point Retreat, as we went into camp one evening, we discovered the body of Peter M. Hansbrough, one of the boatmen drowned on our trip last summer. His remains were easily recognized from the clothing that was still on them. The next morning we buried them under an overhanging cliff. The burial service was brief and simple. We stood around the grave while one short prayer was offered, and we left him with a shaft of pure marble for his headstone, seven hundred feet high, with his name cut upon the base; and in honor of his memory we named a magnificent point opposite — Point Hansbrough."

Leaving this sad story, he picked up his narrative again a while later: "February 5th, we passed Bright Angel Creek, in the Granite Gorge of the Grand Canyon, and on the 6th came to the most powerful and unmanageable rapid we had met on the river. We portaged our supplies, and followed our usual method of swinging the empty boats down by lines. My boat was to go first. The two hundred and fifty foot line was strung out ahead, and the boat was strung into the stream. She rode the huge waves with ease, and went below the rapid without injury. The men and the line worked well and played out smoothly; but when the boat reached the foot of the fall, she acted like a young colt eager for play. She turned her nose out toward the current, and as it struck her, she started like a shot for the other side of the river. The men held to her doggedly. After crossing the current she turned and came back into the eddy, and for a few moments stood still, just as a colt ready for another prance. The men rushed down along the rocks to get the line ahead, but before they could get far enough, she turned her head again to the stream. The men put their wills into their arms and held her once more; she did not cross the current, but on reaching the centre dipped her nose under as if trying her strength, came up at once, rose on a wave, and then, as if for a final effort to gain her liberty, dived her head under, filled with water, and went completely out of sight. In a few moments she rose to the surface, and slowly and leisurely floated sidewise across the eddy toward shore, and quietly stopped alongside a shelving rock. To prevent another such experience we adopted Major Powell's plan in such cases, of shooting the boat through and catching it below. The 'Marie' the rebuilt boat, was started first. She rode gracefully the high waves at the head of the rapid, but in the middle she turned, partially filled with water, shot to one side, struck against the cliff, sank in the worst part of the rapid, and came up in pieces about the size of toothpicks — our five days' labor and our boat gone together!"

Chapter 5: A Series of Great Plateaux

"In local parlance the upper edge of the precipice walls that line the Canyon is called the 'rim.' We never speak of the 'edge' of the Canyon, or the 'banks' of the Colorado River. It is a popular idea that the Canyon is through a country of mountains. This is a mistake. Instead, it cuts through a series of great plateaux, known on the north as the Kaibab, Powell, and Kanab Plateaux, and on the south as the Colorado Plateau. The singularity of this formation is such that one does not discover the existence of this vast waterway, as he journeys northward or southward, until he is on its very brink. Hence, the tremendous and startling surprise that awaits every visitor. The Canyon springs upon him with the leap of a panther, and, suggesting a deserted world, yawns at his feet before he is aware that' he is within miles of it. It overwhelms him by its suddenness, and renders him speechless with its grandeur and magnificence. No reading, no descriptions, no pictures, no warnings can prepare the mind for that one first stupendous, overwhelming impression." - George Wharton James, *In & Around the Grand Canyon*

Kaibab Plateau

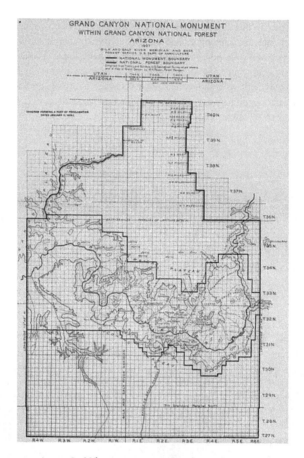

An early 20th century map of the Grand Canyon

By the start of the 20th Century, the Grand Canyon had become a popular destination for ordinary Americans. In 1901, the Atchison, Topeka and Santa Fe Railway opened a branch line to the Grand Canyon Village, a tourist location that had grown up on the South Rim. The first rail passengers arrived there that September.

However, a more important visit came in 1903 when President Theodore Roosevelt toured the area. An avid naturalist, Roosevelt was a major supporter of the movement to preserve important areas as national parks, and while at the Grand Canyon, he gave a speech on May 6 in which he said, "I have come here to see the Grand Canyon of Arizona, because in that canyon Arizona has a natural wonder, which, so far as I know, is in kind absolutely unparalleled throughout the rest of the world. I shall not attempt to describe it, because I cannot. I could not choose words that would convey or that could convey to any outsider what that canyon is. I want you to ask you to do one thing in connection with it in your own interest and in the interest of the country--to keep this great wonder of nature as it now is. I was delighted to learn of the wisdom of the Santa Fe railroad people in deciding not to build their hotel on the brink of the canyon. I hope you will not have a building of any kind, not a summer cottage, a hotel or anything else to mar the wonderful grandeur, the sublimity, the loneliness and beauty of the canyon. Leave it as it is. Man cannot improve on it; not a bit. The ages have been at work on it and man can only mar it. What you can do is to keep it for your children and your children's children and for all who come after you, as one of the great sights which every American, if he can travel at all, should see."

Roosevelt at the Grand Canyon

Roosevelt's speech subsequently set out the groundwork for his plans to make the Grand Canyon National Park. "Keep the Grand Canyon of Arizona as it is. We have gotten past the stage, my fellow citizens, when we are to be pardoned if we simply treat any part of our country as something to be skinned for two or three years for the use of the present generation. Whether it is the forest, the water, the scenery, whatever it is, handle it so that your children's children will get the benefit of it. Handle it that way. If irrigation, apply it under circumstances that will make it of benefit, not to the speculators to get profit out of it for two or three years, but handle it so that it will be of use to the homemaker; to the man who comes to live here and to have his children stay after him; handle it so as to be of use to him and those who come after him. Keep the forests in the same way. Preserve them for that use, but use them so that they will not be squandered; will not be wasted; so that they will be of benefit to the Arizona of 1953 as well as the Arizona of 1903."

Unfortunately, the railroad and other private companies did not pay much attention to Roosevelt's comments on the location of a hotel. When the El Tavor Hotel was built just 20 feet from the rim of the canyon in 1905, it may have spurred Roosevelt's efforts to protect the area; in November 1906, he established the Grand Canyon Game Preserve, and over the next several months, he was able to convince Congress to set aside more land around the canyon until the entire area was made a United States National Monument on January 11, 1908.

Though delays from big business put in off for another decade, the Grand Canyon area was designated a National Park in 1919. The following year, a brochure on the park described the area: "The Grand Canyon National Park is in northern Arizona. Its 958 square miles enclose 56 miles of the Grand Canyon stretching west of its beginning at the mouth of the Marble Canyon. Through it winds the Colorado River. From rim to rim the canyon varies from 8 to 20 miles in width; it is more than a mile deep measured from the north rim, which averages nearly a thousand feet higher than the south rim. The eastern boundary includes the lofty painted walls east of which lies the Painted Desert. Its western boundary includes the broad Cataract Canyon, tributary from the south, in whose depths we find the Havasupai Indian Reservation and a group of fine waterfalls markedly different from any in our other national parks. The park boundaries hug the rim closely. Very little of the country back of the rim is included in the reservation, scarcely enough in places to take care of the great increase of travel which national parkhood will bring to the Grand Canyon during the next several years. These border lands are wonderfully attractive. The northern rim is heavily forested with pine and spruce. The southern rim carries a slender semiarid flowering vegetation of rich beauty and wide variety, and south of the railroad station lie a few square miles of fine yellow pine forest. The Grand Canyon was made a national park in February, 1919, thirty-three years after Benjamin Harrison, then Senator from Indiana, introduced the first of several hills to give it park status. Politics, local apathy, and private interests which sought to utilize its water power and to find minerals in its depths, were the principal causes of delay. All efforts failing to make it a national park, in 1908 President Roosevelt made it a national monument. Once a railroad was surveyed through it. A scenic railroad was projected along its south rim. Less than a year before it became a park, efforts were making in New York to raise money to dam its waters for power and irrigation."

In the mind of the author of the pamphlet, no other wonder in the world compared to the Grand Canyon. While he could easily be accused of being biased, he nonetheless made a good case for his opinion. "There is no doubt that the Grand Canyon is one of the world's very greatest spectacles. It is impossible to compare it with the tremendous white spectacle of the Himalayas, or with the House of Everlasting Fire of the Hawaii National Park, or with the 17,000 feet of snow and glacier which rise abruptly between the observer's eyes and the summit of Mount

McKinley, because it has nothing in common with any of these. But of its own kind there is nothing in the world which approaches it in form, size and glowing color; it is much the greatest example of stream erosion. And in its power to rouse the emotion of the looker-on, to stupefy or to exhilarate, it has no equal of any kind anywhere, unless it be the starry firmament itself. Approaching by rail or road, the visitor comes upon it suddenly. Pushing through the woods from the motor camping ground, or climbing the stairs from the railroad station, it is there at one's feet, disclosed in the sublimity of its templed depths, in the bewildering glory of its gorgeous coloring. There is no preparation of mind and spirit. To some, the revelation is a shock, no matter what the expectation. The rim of the Grand Canyon is one of the stillest places on earth, even when it is crowded with people. To describe the Grand Canyon is as impossible as it is unnecessary. Few natural spectacles have been so fully pictured, few are so familiar even to the untraveled. Its motionless unreality is one of the first and most powerful impressions it makes."

The author then went on to paint a magical picture of what the canyon looked like over the course of a day, and while many would try to lend as good a description, few would succeed. "And yet the Grand Canyon is really a motion picture. There is no moment that it does not change. Always its shadows are insensibly altering, disappearing here, appearing there; lengthening here, shortening there. There is continual movement. With every quarter hour its difference may be measured. There is the Grand Canyon of the early morning, when the light slants lengthwise from the Painted Dessert. The great capes of the northern rim shoot into the picture, outlined in golden light against which their shapes gloom in hazy blues. Certain temples seem to rise slowly from the depths, or to step forward from hiding places in the opposite walls. Down on the green floor the twisting inner gorge discloses here and there lengths of gleaming water, sunlit and yellow. An hour later all is wholly changed. The dark capes have retired somewhat and now are brilliant-hued and thoroughly defined. The temples of the dawn have become remodeled, and scores of others have emerged from the purple gloom. The Granite Gorge, now detailed fully, displays waters which are plainly muddy even at this great distance. And now the opposite wall is seen to be convoluted, possessing many headlands and intervening gulfs. And so, from hour to hour, the spectacle develops. Midday, with sun high behind the south rim, is the time of least charm, for the opposite walls have flattened and the temples of the depths have lost their defining shadows. But as afternoon progresses the spectacles of the morning creep back, now reversed and strangely altered in outline. It is a new Grand Canyon, the some but wonderfully different. And just after sunset the reds deepen to dim purples and the grays and yellows and greens change to magical blues. In the dark of a moonless night the canyon suggests unimaginable mysteries."

Chapter 6: Rocks Beneath

"To discuss exhaustively, in a few pages, the geology of the Grand Canyon, when Major Powell and Captain Button required large volumes for the purpose, is an evident impossibility.

All I can do is to give an outline of their theory. Simultaneous with the deposition of the sedimentary strata in the ocean beds which afterwards became the plateaux of the Grand Canyon region, the uplift and subsidence consequent upon the cooling and contracting of the earth's surface were going on. For it must be remembered that in those early days of the earth's history its crust was in a far more heated, and therefore plastic condition, than it is now. So that when vast sedimentary deposits were rapidly made in any given area, the yielding earth subsided, and thus afforded room for more and higher deposits. These processes of deposition and subsidence continued until, for some reason or other, a new era set in. The depositions ceased, the subsidence was reversed, and uplift began. And ere long (geologically speaking) the matter that had been deposited under water as sand, silt, and what not, now appeared above the face of the waters as solid rock; that latest deposited appearing first. And, if the uplift continues long enough, all the strata thus deposited are exposed, and perhaps also the archaean and plutonic rocks beneath. This is what we actually find to be the case in the Grand Canyon." - George Wharton James, *In & Around the Grand Canyon*

For decades, it was believed that the Grand Canyon was carved by the Colorado River over millions of years, but in the second half of the 20th century, some scientists began to speculate that the Grand Canyon might not be nearly that old. According to a 2000 article in *Science News*, "Scientists later used radioactive dating to determine the ages of layers of the lava and ash that have repeatedly blanketed the area. In the early 1960s, gravel beds atop the plateau and sediments downstream at the mouth of the Colorado River supplied new data about the age and configuration of the area's ancient river systems. In 1964, geologists gathered in Flagstaff, Ariz., to try to assemble these disparate findings into a comprehensive theory of how the canyon came to be. Richard A. Young, now a geologist at the State University of New York in Geneseo, attended the meeting as a graduate student. Young says most of the ideas that came out of that meeting have survived, but new research continues to fill in the blanks and pose additional tantalizing questions about the early days of the Grand Canyon."

Much of the scientists' curiosity related to the shallowest section of the canyon. According to the article, "The lower end of the Grand Canyon is one place that tells researchers just how youthful the mile-deep gorge might be. At that part of the gorge, and about halfway between the surface of the Colorado River and the canyon's rim, lies a band of limestone within sediments that geologists call the Muddy Creek Formation. This layer of white rock, the bottom portions of which gradually blend into the silts and sands of the layer below, is several hundred feet thick and appears on both sides of the canyon. Like other sedimentary rocks, the Muddy Creek Formation is a testament to the environmental conditions in which it formed. Young says the formation's limestone was deposited by types of algae that thrive only in clear, freshwater lakes, suggesting that such a lake once covered the area. The eventual disappearance of the silt and sand from the limestone indicates that the streams that fed the lake gradually began to dry up and carry less sediment. Perhaps, Young notes, this ancient lake in its later years was fed only by springs. Radioactive dating of the many layers of ash in the limestone shows that the lake straddled the area between 6 million and 11 million years ago. This is a critical piece of information, Young says, because it places an age limit on the Grand Canyon. If there was a clear lake with no river delta here 6 million years ago, the muddy Colorado River couldn't have been carving the gorge before that time."

One possible reason why the Grand Canyon developed the way that it did is related to the Colorado River itself. The article pointed out, "Young says this scenario also suggests that the portions of the present-day Colorado River above and below the canyon may not always have been connected. Support for that idea comes from the river delta at the Gulf of California. About 5 microscopic fossils eroded from the Colorado Plateau that are found nowhere else. The most likely explanation for the abrupt appearance of these fossils, Young says, is that a west-flowing tributary of the ancestral lower Colorado River began to carve a small valley eastward into the edge of the Colorado Plateau. The upper portion of the tributary eventually merged with the ancestral upper Colorado River and its tributaries to form a single river system. The result would have been a strengthened torrent of water that could carve its way through rock at a faster clip than ever before. Talk of this scenario began in earnest at the 1964 meeting. 'Fifty years ago, geologists didn't realize how fast erosion could occur,' Young says. 'When there's a depression in the rock and the river flows through, it can erode incredibly rapidly.'"

The article also brought its readers up to date with what had been learned since the first formation of the discussed theories. "At this summer's meeting [in 2000], Young and Francis M. Gough presented data that suggest just how efficiently flowing water can cut into the terrain. About 50 miles south of the Grand Canyon, a small river called West Clear Creek is chewing its way eastward through rocks similar to those that the Colorado began to erode millions of years ago. Even though the river is only 30 miles long and drains an area of just 350 square miles, Young and Gough report that it has carved a canyon 20 miles long in just a few million years. At its mouth, the gorge is the same width and about two-thirds the depth of the Grand Canyon. New data from yet another canyon also show just how fast a river can slash through rock. Robert F. Biek and Grant C. Willis of the Utah Geological Survey in Salt Lake City studied erosion rates along the Virgin River in southwestern Utah, just north of the Grand Canyon. They focused on points both upstream and downstream of the Hurricane Fault, which runs north to south and cuts directly across the river. Using radioactive-dating methods on samples from lava flows and ash beds, the researchers determined the amount of fault movement as well as the rate at which the river chewed downward. Biek and Willis found that over the past million years, the west side of the fault has dropped about 1,300 feet relative to the east side--an average of about 16 inches every 1,000 years. On the east side of the fault, the river has eaten away 16 inches of rock every millennium. In other words, the river has chewed downward on the higher side of the fault to match the river level on the lower side. In a smaller canyon near the Utah-Colorado border, measurements by Biek and Willis showed that the Colorado River has cut through about 360 feet of rock in the past 620,000 years. Downstream in the Grand Canyon, where the Colorado carries much more water and sediment, rates of erosion are likely much higher. It's possible, Young says, that the river carved as much as 1,000 feet of the canyon's depth in the past million years."

Finally, the article concluded by inviting further consideration, as man's understanding of the Grand Canyon, like the Grand Canyon itself, is an ever-evolving thing. "While many presentations at this year's meeting filled in gaps in the 1964 hypothesis of rapid formation of the Grand Canyon, some posed alternative scenarios that could revamp views about the early history of the gorge. For example, circumstantial evidence is mounting that erosion of the gorge could have been started by the floodwaters of a small lake that stood near where the eastern Grand Canyon sits today, says George H. Billingsley, a geologist with the U.S. Geological Survey in Flagstaff. Among other evidence presented at the meeting, the concentration of strontium in a band of sediments found along the lower Colorado River—rocks known as the Bouse Formation--suggests that a lake fed by the ancestral upper Colorado River began to overflow about 5.5 million years ago. After the water broke through the edge of the basin, it spilled across the Colorado Plateau and began to gouge the Grand Canyon, says Norman Meek, a geographer at California State University in San Bernardino. Over the next 1.5 million years, Meek suggests, the resulting flow carved much of the Grand Canyon and other gorges in eastern Arizona. Large amounts of round stone gravel located in the upper portions of the Muddy Creek Formation sediments near the western end of the Grand Canyon provide more support for the overflowing lake scenario. These sediments are now 600 feet thick in places and could be thicker in unexposed areas, says Scott Lundstrom, a Denver-based geologist with the U.S. Geological Survey. The gravel probably was deposited between 4.75 million and 6.9 million years ago, according to radioactive dating of volcanic deposits that sandwich similar layers of gravel just a few miles away. That period corresponds to the era when Meek proposes the lake spilled over, releasing what Lundstrom estimates could have been around 1,000 cubic miles of water. Despite the accumulating data, Billingsley notes that geologists may never be able to verify the early history of their favorite hole in the ground."

Billingsley himself may have summed it up best: "Most of the evidence is gone, because the canyon swallowed the clues to its early history as it grew wider and deeper. It's a puzzle with too many pieces missing. [I hope these findings will get] a whole new generation of students excited."

Online Resources

Yosemite National Park: The History of California's Most Famous Park by Charles River Editors

Yellowstone National Park: The History of America's Most Famous Park by Charles River Editors

Bibliography

Pedro de Castañeda of Najera (1990) [1596]. *The Journey of Coronado, 1540–*

1542 [Originally published as: *Account of the Expedition to Cibola which took place in the year 1540*]. Translated by George Parker Winship. Seville (orig.); Golden, Colorado (trans.): Fulcrum Publishing.

Harris, Ann G.; Tuttle, Esther; Tuttle, Sherwood D. (1997). *Geology of National Parks* (5th ed.). Iowa: Kendall/Hunt Publishing.

James, George. *In & Around the Grand Canyon: The Grand Canyon of the Colorado River in Arizona.* Little Brown. 1908.

Kiver, Eugene P.; Harris, David V. (1999). *Geology of U.S. Parklands* (5th ed.). New York: John Wiley & Sons.

O'Connor, Letitia Burns (1992). *The Grand Canyon*. Los Angeles: Perpetua Press.

Tufts, Lorraine Salem (1998). *Secrets in The Grand Canyon, Zion and Bryce Canyon National Parks* (3rd ed.). North Palm Beach, Florida: National Photographic Collections.

CPSIA information can be obtained
at www.ICGtesting.com
Printed in the USA
BVHW01s2139111217
502558BV00009B/181/P